THE NEXT GOAT

CAITLIN CLARK

CORINA JEFFRIES

PowerKiDS press

Published in 2025 by The Rosen Publishing Group, Inc.
2544 Clinton Street, Buffalo, NY 14224

First Edition

Editor: Greg Roza
Book Design: Rachel Rising

Photo Credits: Cover, pp. 11, 17, 21 ASSOCIATED PRESS/AP Images; Cover, pp. 1, 3 ,4, 6, 8,10, 12, 14, 16, 18, 20, 22, 23, 24 Pixacon/Shutterstock.com; Cover, Farhanz9/Shutterstock.com; Cover, p. 1 Alhovik/Shutterstock.com; pp. 5, 7, 13 ZUMA Press, Inc./Alamy Stock Photo; p. 6 mipan/Shutterstock.com; p. 9 Michael Allio/Icon Sportswire 2024; p. 10 focal point/Shutterstock.com; p. 12 https://commons.wikimedia.org/wiki/File:Iowa_Hawkeyes_wordmark.svg; p. 14 Alter-ego/Shutterstock.com; p. 15 https://commons.m.wikimedia.org/wiki/File:Iowa_Hawkeyes_B1G_champions_(52757660611).jpg;
p. 16 https://commons.wikimedia.org/wiki/File:WNBA_logo.png; p. 19 Sipa USA/Alamy Stock Photo.

Library of Congress Cataloging-in-Publication Data

Names: Jeffries, Corina, author.
Title: Caitlin Clark / Corina Jeffries.
Description: Buffalo : PowerKids Press, 2025. | Series: The next GOAT | Includes index.
Identifiers: LCCN 2024026552 (print) | LCCN 2024026553 (ebook) | ISBN 9781499449617 (library binding) | ISBN 9781499449600 (paperback) | ISBN 9781499449624 (ebook)
Subjects: LCSH: Clark, Caitlin, 2002–Juvenile literature. | Women basketball players–United States–Biography–Juvenile literature. | Basketball players–United States–Biography–Juvenile literature. | Iowa Hawkeyes (Women's basketball team)–Juvenile literature.
Classification: LCC GV884.C554 J44 2025 (print) | LCC GV884.C554 (ebook) | DDC 796.323092 [B]–dc23/eng/20240627
LC record available at https://lccn.loc.gov/2024026552
LC ebook record available at https://lccn.loc.gov/2024026553

Manufactured in the United States of America

CPSIA Compliance Information: Batch #CWPK25. For Further Information contact Rosen Publishing at 1-800-237-9932.

CONTENTS

MEET CAITLIN!

Caitlin Clark is one of the greatest college basketball players of all time. During her four years with the University (college) of Iowa Hawkeyes, Clark scored 3,951 points. That's the record for both women *and* men's **Division I** college basketball! This is just one of her many college accomplishments.

Clark is a point guard known for making three-point shots. Now she's proving her basketball skills in the Women's National Basketball Association (WNBA). Although she's just started playing **professional** basketball, many people are expecting greatness.

WHAT THEY'RE SAYING

"[Clark] has raised the excitement of our sport . . . . She does things in a different way than anybody else can do."
—Lisa Bluder, Iowa Hawkeyes coach (2000–2024)

Clark is one of the best three-point shooters the game has ever seen. She's well known for sinking "long threes," or shots very far from the basket.

A NATURAL TALENT

Clark was born in Des Moines, Iowa, on January 22, 2002. She grew up in Des Moines in a family that loved watching and playing sports. Her father, Brent, played college baseball and basketball. Her brother, Blake, played football at Iowa State University.

When Clark was just 5 years old, she could **dribble** a basketball! Clark was also very **competitive** as a child, especially with two big brothers! She quickly picked up the skills needed to be the best.

Caitlin celebrates with her mom Anne and father Brent at the 2024 Women's NCAA Tournament. Clark helped Iowa reach second place.

IOWA MISS BASKETBALL

When she was young, Clark played on boys' youth basketball teams. She also played volleyball, soccer, and softball. Clark attended Dowling Catholic High School in West Des Moines. During her first two years, she played soccer and basketball. She was the leading scorer on the soccer team! However, Clark decided to play basketball for her last two years in high school.

When she finished high school in 2020, Clark was one of Iowa's leading basketball players. Iowa sports reporters named her Iowa Miss Basketball.

WHAT THEY'RE SAYING

Even before her first high school game, a college coach called Clark's high school coach Kristin Meyer. "They told me she could play for them right now," Meyer recalled.

During a high school game in 2019, Clark scored 60 points for the Dowling Maroons!

WORLD CHAMP

In 2017, USA Basketball invited Clark to join the under-16 U.S. national basketball team. She helped the team come in first place during the Women's Americas **Championship**.

In 2019 and 2021, Clark played for the under-19 U.S. women's national basketball team. She competed with other young players from around the word. The under-19 U.S. women's team won first place for both championships, bringing Clark's gold medal count to 3—before she was even 19 years old! Clark won the most **valuable** player award for the 2021 championship.

Clark hopes to represent the United States at the Summer Olympic Games in the near future.

THE IOWA HAWKEYES

After high school, Clark decided to attend the University of Iowa (UI). The Iowa Hawkeyes play in a league call the Big Ten. The Big Ten is a Division I league, meaning it's filled with the top players.

Clark had an instant effect on the team in her first year! She started 30 games and led the country in points scored, total **assists**, three-pointers, and **field goals**. Clark was named the Big Ten's Freshman (first season) of the Year for the 2020–2021 season.

Clark improved as she got older. During her second year at UI, she became the fastest player in Big Ten history to reach 1,000 points.

COLLEGE STAR

In 2024, Clark played in one of the greatest games of her college career. The Hawkeyes played the University of Nebraska Cornhuskers in the Big Ten championship game. The Hawkeyes beat the Cornhuskers 94–89 to win the championship. Clark won the Big Ten Player of the Year award for the third year in a row.

During the Big Ten **Tournament** in 2024, Clark set the record for the most three-point shots made in a season with 201. This bested the past Division I recordholder—NBA great Stephen Curry.

WHAT THEY'RE SAYING

"[Clark's] shooting ability is her superpower, but the rest of her game is as polished as that."
— Stephen Curry, four-time NBA champion

Clark ended her college career with many Division I women's basketball records, including most career points, highest scoring average, most three-pointers per game, and much more!

THE WNBA DRAFT

Although the Hawkeyes reached the NCAA tournament three years in a row, they never won a championship. However, Clark's college play was nothing short of amazing. With numbers like Clark's, she was sure to be a hit in the WNBA.

After college, Clark was the best player in the WNBA **draft**. Many players and coaches wanted to add her to their teams. They knew Clark was a great shooter, especially from far away. The Indiana Fever selected Clark as the top pick in the draft!

WNBA

Clark holds up her jersey for the Indiana Fever shortly after being drafted first overall.

THE INDIANA FEVER

The WNBA was founded in 1996. The Indiana Fever have been a WNBA team since 2000. They won the WNBA Championship in 2012. The Fever have struggled in recent years, and they didn't make the playoffs between 2017 and 2023.

However, now the Fever have Clark on the team! Clark's presence has increased the sales of WNBA tickets as new fans flock to see her play in the pros. The style of play in the WNBA is tougher than college. Most fans think it's only a matter of time before Clark raises her game and becomes the next GOAT!

On July 6, 2024, during a game between the Fever and the New York Liberty, Clark had a total of 19 points, 12 **rebounds**, and 13 assists. That's called a "triple-double," and Clark is the first WNBA rookie ever to get one!

WHAT'S NEXT FOR CAITLIN?

Hopes are very high for Caitlin Clark. Many people consider her the greatest female player ever to play college basketball. She's as good shooting the ball as she is blocking other players from scoring. Only time will tell if Clark's the next WNBA GOAT.

Many people expect Clark to do well in the WNBA. But Clark hopes to one day play on the U.S. women's national team in the Olympics. Clark said, "Being able to [play basketball] on the highest level would certainly be a dream come true."

WHAT THEY'RE SAYING

"I knew in my heart here that what we've been able to do [at Iowa] is so special, and that it's not over yet, but I think I'm ready for the next chapter in my life, too."
—**Caitlin Clark**

Fans are sure to keep watching as Clark improves her game and strives for greatness in the WNBA.

GLOSSARY

assist: The action of a player who, by passing a ball, makes it possible for a teammate to score a field goal.

championship: The end game in a sport season, determining the overall winner.

competitive: Having a strong desire to win or be the best at something.

Division I: The highest level of college sports in the United States.

draft: A process of selecting young players to be members of the teams in a league.

dribble: To bounce a basketball.

field goal: In basketball, a basket made from anywhere on the court during play.

professional: Related to something people do for money.

rebound: When a player grabs the ball after a missed shot.

tournament: A contest or series of contests played for a championship.

valuable: Important.

FOR MORE INFORMATION

BOOKS

Hewson, Anthony K. *Caitlin Clark: Basketball Superstar.* Mendota Heights, MN: North Star Editions, 2024.

O'Neal, Ciara. *The WNBA Finals.* Mendota Heights, MN: Apex, 2023.

Whiting, Jim. *The Story of the Indiana Fever.* Mankato, MN: Creative Paperbacks, 2024.

WEBSITES

The Indiana Fever
fever.wnba.com
You can learn more about the Fever and Caitlin Clark on the official Fever webpage.

Women's National Basketball Association (WNBA)
www.wnba.com
Check out the latest scores and news stories from the WNBA.

Publisher's note to educators and parents: Our editors have carefully reviewed these websites to ensure that they are suitable for students. Many websites change frequently, however, and we cannot guarantee that a site's future contents will continue to meet our high standards of quality and educational value. Be advised that students should be closely supervised whenever they access the internet.

INDEX